THE COLOR OF LIGHT

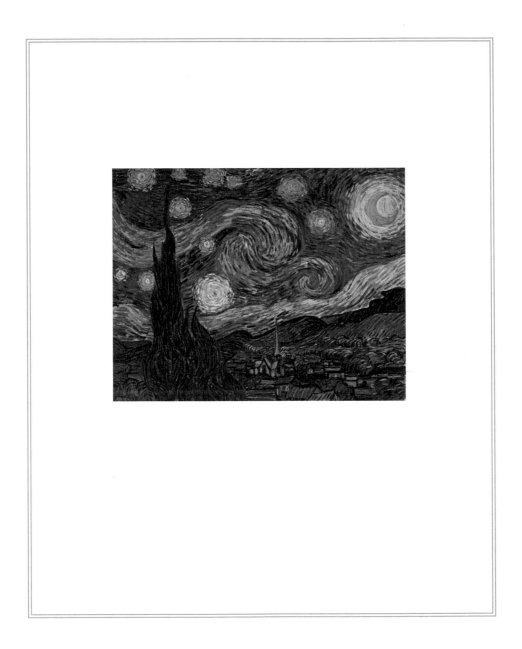

The Color of Light

Poems on Van Gogh's Late Paintings

MARILYN CHANDLER MCENTYRE

WILLIAM B. EERDMANS PUBLISHING COMPANY
GRAND RAPIDS, MICHIGAN / CAMBRIDGE, U.K.

THE COLOR OF LIGHT
Poems on Van Gogh's Late Paintings

Text copyright © 2007 by Marilyn Chandler McEntyre
Published 2007 by Wm. B. Eerdmans Publishing Company
2140 Oak Industrial Drive NE, Grand Rapids, Michigan 49505 /
P.O. Box 163, Cambridge CB3 9PU U.K.
Printed in the U.S.A.
11 10 09 08 07   7 6 5 4 3 2 1

Library of Congress Cataloging-in-Publication Data
McEntyre, Marilyn Chandler, 1949–
    The color of light: poems on Van Gogh's late paintings / Marilyn Chandler McEntyre.
      p. cm.
    ISBN 978-0-8028-2728-9 (alk. paper)
    1. Gogh, Vincent van, 1853–1890—Poetry. 2. Painting—Poetry. I. Title.

PS3563.C3616C65 2007
811'.54—dc22

2007023129

Book designed by Willem Mineur

www.eerdmans.com

Acknowledgments

I am grateful to those who have read and listened along the way,
encouraged me in my habits of musing, and talked to me
about art: Tony Askew, Susan Savage, and Logan Speirs,
who make the stretched canvas into sacred space;
Paul Willis, faithful steward of words and generous reader;
Deborah and George, whose friendship feeds my spirit.
I am grateful to each beloved person in our extended family
for the points of view and ways of seeing that surprise
and teach me, especially to Jordan, Jared, and Shona,
who continue to offer me new vantage points, and
to Mary, Elizabeth, and Margaret, who share in my life
and work and interior conversation in more ways
than they know.

And, as always, I am grateful to my husband John, who walks
with me at the water's edge and helps me see the color of light.

THE COLOR OF LIGHT

Table of Contents

Introduction

VAN GOGH'S 1886 "Self-Portrait with Gray Felt Hat" shows a man with a gaze of iconic intensity. Light falls on him like rain, flecks his brown coat and lines his hat's edge. As in so many of the artist's later works, the boundary between matter and energy blurs: light gathers into the density of human form at an intersection of time and space, surprising and provisional. In "Self-Portrait with Straw Hat," painted a year later, the solidity of body and borders has almost given way to ambient air, sun-filled and dappled with blue, dense as the stuff of straw and skin. Shocking blue eyes peer at the viewer from somewhere just beyond the frequencies we inhabit. The line of solid red that marks his shirt's edge seems a vestige of what, all around it, has been reabsorbed.

By one means or another, Van Gogh invites us to see the light we dwell in. The shimmering sliver of moonlight on water, the last red gleam of sunset, the color of a cat's fur in lamplight, the circle cast by a candle in a dark room — these call our attention to what is all around us and can be apprehended only by indirection. Sometimes an epiphany occurs: a bush burns, a pillar of fire appears, there is a transfiguration. There are reports of angels and apparitions. Sometimes our merely human love allows us moments of seeing what we rightly call radiance. Mostly, though, we content ourselves with the categories of solid, liquid, and gas, and with the borders and edges that mark off the things of this world into what is numerable, describable, and safe. Only the occasional artist (or particle physicist) threatens the dogmas of the unaided senses and ambushes us with truths that disturb the universe. With the aid of a paintbrush (or an electron microscope), we see in new dimensions.

Poets resort to metaphor. When the Psalmist speaks of mountains clapping their hands, of leaping waters, and of rocks crying out, it is to testify to a truth that must be told "slant," as Emily Dickinson put it, and must "dazzle gradually, or every man be blind." Artists set themselves a similar task: to tell some truth that lifts us into a place of awareness just beyond the comfort zone of convention, just a little to the left of what is safe and acceptable. Van Gogh's paintings dazzle gradually. They leave a remarkable record of a visionary journey that emerges from the darkness of coal mines and Flemish winters to the sun and wind of southern France, where mass and color are reorganized in a shocking revaluation of weight, density, refraction, and movement. Light scatters, diffuses, or gathers into thick yellow strokes that give the sun unnerving solidity. The rumbling yellow of Van Gogh's last wheat field, painted in the month he died, stands out against a lowering sky with a vitality that defies the ambient darkness. Color itself, the gift of light broken for us into endlessly recombinant shades and tones, offered him a way out of anxious uncertainties into the bold, bright declarations of a man who heard his calling and said yes.

And he left us the same invitation: say yes. The paintings call for our consent — to relinquish, to reorganize, to reimagine, to see into, to see through. To let solid objects be verbs rather than nouns and to recognize the surging life force in an olive tree or a bank of wild iris urgent with the work of growing purple. If you soften your vision just a little and let your eye relax into submission, you may get a glimpse of the "unified field" where forces come together and negotiate their differences in intimate and energetic play.

The intimacy can be appalling, or at least intimidating. In a poem simply entitled "Van Gogh," Jeanne Murray Walker imagines how the artist spoke "straight into the ear of God." All of his work is relational, even con-frontational. Not only portraits but landscapes, skyscapes, the crowds in the marketplace come to him, and through him, as personal encounter. The ques-tion that seems to lie behind them is large and radically theological: Who is this that speaks and shines in all that may be seen? It may be a vision of the One Hopkins described, who "fathers forth, whose beauty is past change." It may be the One the sight of whose face cannot be borne.

Evidently something in the light Van Gogh saw became unbearable. The sorrows of his solitude, the episodes of derangement, and finally his suicide infuse his story with what Unamuno called "a tragic sense of life": something mighty and rich with spiritual vitality fell when he died. What he left us cost him "not less than everything." Hardly a chronicle of spiritual clarity or conversion in any conventional sense, Van Gogh's story still has a place in the lineage of seers, mystics, poets, and priests who have attempted to mediate what comes to them in moments of greatest attunedness and make it available to the eyes and ears of others who are finding their way out of Plato's cave. We are called by the Light into the light we can't yet bear without the shades and protections of mud, mortar, wood, canvas, and color. Art is a form of mercy that meets us where we are with what is hospitable and familiar, made only a little strange to stretch us toward what can't be seen with the naked eye or fully understood, but recognized and claimed if we assent to what is offered.

The poems in this volume, meditations on the paintings of Van Gogh's final difficult, spiritually strenuous years, are my acts of assent. They are not scholarly comment, but simply thanks for a costly gift freely given that has afforded me, among so many others, challenges and opportunities to look again and see in a new light.

MARILYN CHANDLER MCENTYRE

Self-Portrait with Gray Felt Hat

(1886/87)

There were winters of discontent;
money was scarce and hunger
only thinly disguised by decent
attire. Still, even the darkest
day that December offered
its tithe of color — muted
yellow and soft green-gray lent
their energies to his practice
of presence.

And the face — the face,
where red-orange flickers defiant
against what damps and dulls,
draws to itself all available
light. A long, slow burning
keeps it alive like a vigil lamp,
trimmed and watchful
in the cavernous dark.

Van Gogh's Bedroom

(1888)

Just what you need in a room:
a window tall enough for poplars,
bright with borrowed green;
crookedness and color enough
to keep the eye entertained.

You need a pitcher and pegs
and an empty vase ready for sunflowers
or irises when you can get them.

If the blanket is red enough,
you will sleep the sleep
of the living, the restless energies
of afternoon funneling into dream;
and if your pillows are yellow, you will not
forget how sun lit the tips of grass
like candles and made long fingers
of light in the roadway.

You need two chairs, even if
company never comes, because
they might. They might, still —
a brother, someone from Paris.

And paintings — portraits for remembrance
and landscapes — because
it is not good for man to be enclosed
or kept too long from where everything
that lives offers him air.

And a mirror for truth. Every day it delivers
its ephemeral record of change like headlines:
"Unshaven artist finds new hope." "Old loss leaves
belated mar." "New shades come out at first light."

You need angles and corners and a floor rough enough
to help the feet remember the honesties of earth.

And two doors are good: one for welcome, one for retreat,
though the way in and the way out are the same.

Entrance to the Public Gardens in Arles

(1888)

We do what we can to domesticate
the rioting color, sweep the walkways
down to a uniform yellow and circle
flower and foliage with iron wrought
in their image. We make spaces for sitting,
paths for solitude, gateways that mark what we leave,
what we enter. We shape the wild that stirs us despite
ourselves into troubling confluent memories of
something older and darker where once we were lost
in the middle of life's way.

Portrait

of

Joseph

Roulin

(1888)

What you remember are the whiskers.
The hat, the label, the cross-hatched uniform
give him rank and office — but the whiskers
stick out, angular, bold and bushy, his only vanity,
the only thing he sees in the small, fading mirror
that hangs over a pitcher and bowl where every
morning he trims a few stray hairs before walking
his route through Arles, bearing news, being
a local landmark, taking stock with eyes inured
to harsh Provençal sun, from behind the remarkable
beard that quietly defies diminishment.

The Sower

(1888)

You have to get there just as
the grass turns blue, just when
two birds come to glean
and the sun has begun its
vesper song over the hum
of the wheatfield. You have to
keep your distance; the sower
is at prayer. The swing
of his arm and the long stride
turn old parables to chant —

Some seed fell underfoot,
some seed fell on the rock,
some seed fell among thorns,
some seed fell on good soil.
These are the kingdom's secrets.
He who has ears, listen —

taking no more thought as he sings
than the birds who hover
among the furrows,
casting their shadows
on the burning air.

The Rocks

(1888)

We honor what survives. Out of rocky earth
where the grasses wither even as they grow
and the rising tree bends almost to breaking,
where color itself is spare, and the energies
of a wild and hungry palette give way to ascetic
pale, something still says yes to the upward pull,
and stretches into shape. Rocks curve like
the turtle's back. They make their slow way.
The acquiescent tree still gives forth its shade of green.

Portrait
of
Madame
Trabuc

(1889)

If you only saw the lavender around her,
how she parts the light into blue and pink
and bits of yellow, you might remember
how once she sang and her hair fell free,
how she walked the fields and gathered
flowers that grandchildren bring her now
to wear to town. She has been whittled
and planed, smoothed and hollowed by sorrow,
borne it with dignity and dark dresses, but still
there is the lavender light, and an eye that watches
for what it might catch and keep to feed her
heart when she unpins her hair and lies down
to wakefulness in the long provincial night.

Irises

(1889)

Irises on the corner table, still standing
discreet and tall after three days,
remind me of Van Gogh's.

These, though, are not rampant
or entangled, as though life underground
had been an orgy of shared nitrogen,
winding roots, and worms. The yellow V
of their open petals is demure, unlike
the irises of Arles, whose yellow centers
protrude like tongues, bare and bawdy.

They sway and sing their blowsy blues
as yellow and white choirs sing backup,
so loud with life it echoes still in purple fields.

Landscape with House and Ploughman

(1889)

Colors camouflage a light so generous it lets itself
be broken again and again into seven shades
of rainbow and then again to
ochre and rust and slate,
magenta and red rich as blood.

How can the ploughman know what he inhabits?
The world he works in, burrow and
groove and slope, holds him secure and
sets his course, anchored behind
the plough. Unless God gave him some

good reason to climb this hill,
why would he ever see what stretches
and sighs, curved and luxurious
in afternoon sun? Why watch
the day pass over the land,
leaving horse and plough, serving
no earthly purpose?

The

Olive Trees

(1889)

If the sun came closer,
everything would burn.
Each tree is an act of courage,
holding its own, making peace
with the heat and dry ground,
forbearing while mountains,
not yet made low, rise like
monuments to what may be borne.

God, who burned in bush and pillar,
watches still from behind a veil of fire,
burns away, and scatters in harsh
and unavoidable blessing. Under its heat
the small fruit grow, are plucked and brought
to vinegar and salt. Immolation
brings forth. Taste and see.

Cypresses

(1889)

Everything moves upward:
earth into water, air, and finally
fire that burns up, up, energy so
refined that it baffles the bounding senses.

What must it be to see the urgency
of the cypress, and how the very field
strains higher, envying the clouds,
loving the early moon, roots tingling
in earth that will not let them go?

But the form of this life
is a calling and a command:
accept it all — the cells, the helix,
the twist and spin of whorled bark,
the partial death, yellow to brown. Even
clouds consent for a while to curl
and thicken, and the moon wanes
into a dense ridge, distilled before
it dies. These are the terms
the lilies get. They toil not,
but they spin, they spin.

Mountains
at
Saint-Rémy
(1889)

Faith will move mountains.
See how they roll and wind
among the little trees?

Where once they slid into rubble,
rock face stares out over the valley,
unabashed as revelation.

If you say to them, "Jump,"
if you say it as a prayer, you will see
how they already leap with joy,
how their hands clap, how
they do not need you to see them
there, under the eye of God.

At their edges, where the wind blows,
where the dust rises and the light falls,
they rustle softly and turn to sky.

Poplars

at

Saint-Rémy

(1889)

This from an asylum window:
The sky is dark.
The poplars lean,
uncertain among broken
rocks, and a path tacks uphill
toward God. The light
is distant, thin, and fleeting.
Dark grows thick at the edges,
and at the core where trunk meets branch.
The yellows rust. What time we may
in him behold is late in the year, late.
But nothing is like the light here at the verge
of darkness. It took a pilgrimage
to see it just this way.

The

Starry Night

(1889)

What laughter booms across the night sky
from the bellies of heavenly beings? Few hear it,
but sometimes the breath of heaven curls like a bard's beard
and what has only twinkled begins to beat and throb.

Behind it all a drumbeat calls over the mountains.
The villagers think it's thunder, those who are not asleep.
Only a few remain awake to see the starry, starry night
and witness what they can barely imagine how to tell.

Some nights the roar breaks the silence. One was there
when it happened, and saw, and tried to tell the secret,
and died young. How much of life he gave for this
we cannot know. We know only that something precious
as nard was poured out at the foot of these hills,
the blue, the yellow bought with solitary tears.

Couple
Walking
between
Rows
of Trees

(1890)

Just beyond where the shadows begin
to seem like endless night, light
filters through leaves and falls
like lace on the forest floor.

Out of the darkness they come
upon flowers in such prodigal beauty,
even the pathway is overgrown
and scented like a bridal chamber.

They walk slowly, lingering
in the half-light where memory
of darkness endured competes
with the seductions of spring,

glad for companionship and careful
not to say too much. They know
what love costs. What has died fuels
and feeds all that lives. To choose life

on hard terms, to consent
again to hope takes
a little time. But sunlight, dappling
all they see, invites them on.

The

Cottages

(1890)

Houses verge into hill
as smoke becomes sky
and soil runs, flowers,
and flows downward
from crest to canyon.

How brave the brightness
of tile roofs, the borders
of gardens, precarious
at this angle, but clinging
and thriving under
windows where a cheerful
eye watches them into
ripeness. It is all
quickened under a sky
growing denser with time.

Though larger things
are afoot, the hearth
will be tended and the dead
branches trimmed.

Morning: Going Out to Work

(after Millet: 1890)

It would not occur to them that they are seen. Hardly
objects at all, they are the rhythm of the rising day.
Hooves and shoes measure minutes that need
no clocks but gather into hours at the ends
of the furrows, among the flowers, and spill
and pool in the shade under haystacks.

Each receives the morning's blessing on backs
not yet bent over the yielding earth. Quiet
serves as well as speech; what they require
of one another needs few words.

In the pitch of his fork there is rest, and in the arm
that lies on her empty basket. You rest when
you can. You go slowly. You enter each morning
into obedience to the earth that is the Lord's.
You follow the donkey into a story
as old as deserts and salvation.

Noon

Rest

(after Millet: 1890)

To rest before the sheaves are bound,
toss the scythes aside, bare the feet and sink
into the nearest haystack, release
the undone task and consent to sleep
while the brightest hour burns an arc
across its stretch of sky:
this is the body's prayer, mid-day angelus
whispered in mingled breath while the limbs
stretch in thanksgiving and the body turns
toward the beloved.

This is the prayer of trust:
what's left undone will wait. The unattended
child, the uncut acre, cracked wheel, broken
fence that are occupations of the waking mind
soften into shadow in the semi-darkness
of dream. All shall be well. Little depends on us.
The turning world is held and borne in love.
We give good measure in our toil and, meet and right,
obey the body when it calls us to rest.

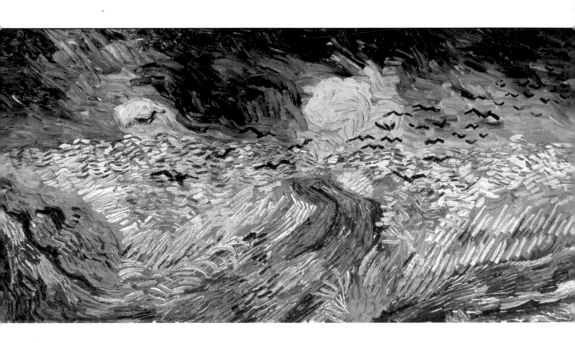

Wheatfield with Crows

(1890)

Suddenly crows, shaken
out of a lowering sky,
stretch dark wings
over wind-bent stalks,
searching out the hidden
seed, now past protection.
Wheel tracks leave
their scar where once
a steward came and paused
and saw that all was well.
He sleeps now, awaiting
harvest, and does not see
how the clouds darken
just here, and how the wheat,
grown and golden, and the tares,
too, face a sky with seven
vials tipped and ready. After
the birds, the horsemen
come. Already the earth
shakes. But the sun
that poured itself, day
after day into these stalks,
shines. It shines.

Self-Portrait with Straw Hat

(1887)

The many colors of Vincent's face
dapple in undulant sunlight.
Every pockmarked plane
lets new light play.

Under the hat's brim blue eyes
burn and bore into air until
it yields its fire. Sleepless nights
have filled them with stars.

A crown of yellow, a halo
of straw sets him apart.
Noonday sweat, like an anointing,
leaves its glistening trace.

It is not self he sees splayed
on the mirror's surface — only
light gathered into flesh for one
kaleidoscopic hour under the sun.

What Happened When He Looked

His miners are made of earth, his sowers so close
to the color of the fields, only the broad hat, the sack,
the outflung arm keeps them from fading into wheat.

But sometimes, he found, the earth itself turns
to water. Mountains tumble like rapids, waves
curling, blue, roiling and leaping like
the Psalmist's mountains clapping their hands.

And water turns to air. As life turns to breath.
The sky grows heavy with sun and draws
everything into its fierce embrace, urging
matter upward and homeward to where
the energies of earth begin.

And then there is fire. When they are alive enough
(or we), bushes burn. If you see it, you go
reeling home along a roadway you suddenly know
is temporary and might evaporate or begin
to pinwheel around a star, taking you with it
beyond deeper and deeper blue, into yellow that melts
to a core of thick, transparent white where love
burns day and night to fuel the fallen seed.

LIST OF ILLUSTRATIONS

Page 36: *Mountains at Saint-Rémy*, c. July 1889. Oil on canvas, 71.8 x 90.8 cm. Solomon R. Guggenheim Museum, New York, NY. Thannhauser Collection, Gift of Justin K. Thannhauser, 1978, 78.2514.24.

Page 38: *Poplars at Saint-Rémy*, c. 1889. Oil on fabric, 61.6 x 45.7cm. © The Cleveland Museum of Art. Bequest of Leonard C. Hanna Jr. 1958.32.

Page 40: *The Starry Night*, c. 1889. Oil on canvas, 29 x 36¼ inches. Acquired through the Lillie P. Bliss Bequest (472.1941). The Museum of Modern Art, New York, NY. Digital Image © The Museum of Modern Art/Licensed by Scala/Art Resource, NY.

Page 42: *Undergrowth with Two Figures*, c. 1890. Cincinnati Art Museum. Bequest of Mary E. Johnston, Accession # 1967.1430.

Page 44: *Cottages with Thatched Roofs*, c. 1890. Hermitage, St. Petersburg, Russia. Photo credit: Scala/Art Resource, NY.

Page 46: *Morning: Going Out to Work* (after Millet), c. 1890, The State Hermitage Museum, St. Petersburg, Russia.

Page 48: *La Meridienne* or *La Sieste*; or *Noon Rest* (after Millet), c. 1889-90. Oil on canvas, 73 x 91 cm. Musee d'Orsay, Paris, France. Photo credit: Erich Lessing/Art Resource, NY.

Page 50: *Wheatfield with Crows*, c. 1890. Van Gogh Museum, Amsterdam, The Netherlands. Photo credit: Art Resource, NY.

Page 52: *Self-Portrait with Straw Hat and Artist's Smock*, c. 1887. Oil on cardboard, 46 x 53 cm. Van Gogh Museum, Amsterdam, The Netherlands (Vincent van Gogh Foundation).

Page 55: Detail of *Self-Portrait with Straw Hat*.